This book belongs to

Montanna

Rea

Wilkinson

$$\begin{array}{r} 2\!\!\!/14 \\ -\ 1\ 7 \\ \hline 0\ 7 \end{array}$$

$$\begin{array}{r} 1 \\ 2\!\!\!/9 \\ -\ 1\ 9 \\ \hline 2\!0 \end{array}$$

$$\begin{array}{r} 6 \\ 7\,9 \\ 4\,0 \\ \hline 2\,9 \end{array}$$

tiger tales

an imprint of ME Media, LLC

202 Old Ridgefield Road, Wilton, CT 06897

Published in the United States 2003

Originally published as Op slot in Belgium 2001

By Uitgeverij Clavis, Amsterdam–Hasselt

Copyright ©Uitgeverij Clavis, Amsterdam–Hasselt

CIP data is available

ISBN 1-58925-378-7

Printed in Hong Kong

1 3 5 7 9 10 8 6 4 2

Anna's Tight Squeeze

by
Marian De Smet

Illustrated by
Marja Meijer

tiger tales

It's Wednesday, the day Mom and Anna always go to the library. The first thing Anna does is return all her books from last week to the lady at the desk and then quickly chooses five new ones.

But Mom is taking a long time, like she *always* does.

Anna is bored waiting for Mom
to look for her books.
   "Come on, Mom,"
Anna whines.
   "Just a minute honey,"
Mom good-naturedly
replies.
   "Mom, I have to go to the
bathroom," she whispers.
   But Mom is busy reading
and doesn't hear her.
"Mmhmm," sighs Mom.

"I'll just go quickly then," Anna mumbles as she walks away. She goes to the bathroom door with the picture of the girl on it.

Inside the bathroom, Anna eyes the
door's lock and handle. Mom doesn't like
Anna to lock the door from the inside, so
Anna checks the lock carefully.

After she flushes the toilet, Anna reaches for the door. She turns the handle. *Click, clack.* It's stuck! She keeps trying. *Click, clack! Click, clack!*

Next Anna tugs at the door. . . . Then she tries pushing the door. But nothing seems to work. It won't open. She tries to turn the handle again and again, but it's still stuck. *Now what?!*

Anna notices that the door doesn't reach to the floor. So she tries to crawl under it. It's a tight squeeze! But she doesn't quite fit. And when she pulls her feet up from under the door, she discovers one of her shoes has fallen off. *Oh no!*

Anna lies on her stomach and reaches for her shoe on the other side of the door, but she can't quite grab it.

Anna takes off her coat and tries to crawl under the door again, this time with her head first.

Oooof! No, that doesn't work either. Her head is just too big.

Then Anna tries to climb over the top of the door. But it's no use. She's just not tall enough.

Suddenly, a boy's face appears from under the door.

"This is the girls' room," Anna says. "Boys have to use the other one."

"Does this shoe belong to you?" the boy asks.

"Oh, yes," Anna says. "Thanks." Then she tells the boy, "The door is stuck. I can't get out of the bathroom."

"Can't you crawl under the door?" the boy asks.

"No," says Anna with a huff. "Can you open the door?"

The boy's head disappears.

Anna can hear the boy jiggling the door handle.
"This side of the door only has the handle," he says.
"I can't move the knob from here to unlock it."

"Come over to my side," Anna says.

"How?" the boy asks.

"Can *you* crawl under the door?"
Anna asks. "I'll help you."

"Ouch, ouch, ouch," the boy says as
he wriggles under the door.

The boy tries to turn the handle from
the inside, but he can't do it either.

"It's broken," he says.

The boy sits down on the closed toilet seat. "I'm Peter," he says.

"And I'm Anna," Anna replies. "What are we going to do while we're stuck in here?"

Peter takes one of Anna's books and she sits down next to him. Together they read the books Anna's chosen while they wait for someone to find them.

All of a sudden, Anna hears her name. Anna peeks
under the door and sees Mom's shoes right in front of her.
"Mom, I'm here! In the bathroom!"

Mom bends down to talk to Anna under the door. "I was worried sick," Mom says. "Why didn't you tell me you were going to the bathroom?"

"I did tell you," Anna mumbles.

"And you know you aren't supposed to lock the door," Mom says.

"The lock is broken," Peter explains.

"Who is that?" asks Mom.

"That's my new friend Peter," Anna replies.

Anna's mom looks through her bag. With a nail file she jiggles the lock on the door. A screw falls on the floor. The handle moves up and down and...the door opens.

Mom helps Anna with her coat. "Thanks Mom," sighs Anna. "Can we go home now?"

"Just as soon as I use the bathroom, too," says Mom. "Here, Anna, please hold my books for a minute."

Mom disappears behind the door. "Wait right here," she says.

A few minutes later the handle moves up and down. And then again…

Anna hears thumping from the other side of the bathroom door.

"Honey," Mom calls, "go get the librarian at the front desk. The door won't open."

Anna laughs. "Mom," she says, "you know you shouldn't lock the door!"

And while Anna is running to get the librarian,
Peter pushes a book under the door…

Explore the world of tiger tales!

Laura's Star
by Klaus Baumgart
ISBN 1-58925-374-4

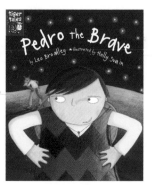

Pedro the Brave
by Leo Broadley
illustrated by Holly Swain
ISBN 1-58925-375-2

More fun-filled and exciting stories await you!
Look for these titles and more at your local library or bookstore.
And have fun reading!

tiger tales
202 Old Ridgefield Road, Wilton, CT 06897

Snarlyhissopus
by Alan MacDonald
illustrated by Louise Voce
ISBN 1-58925-370-1

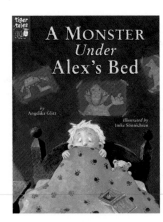

A Monster Under Alex's Bed
by Angelika Glitz
illustrated by Imke Sönnichsen
ISBN 1-58925-373-6

Commotion in the Ocean
by Giles Andreae
illustrated by David Wojtowycz
ISBN 1-58925-366-3

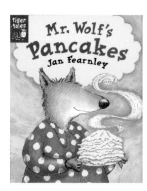

Mr. Wolf's Pancakes
by Jan Fearnley
ISBN 1-58925-354-X